GRADUATES

JEFF ATWOOD

HARVEST HOUSE PUBLISHERS
EUGENE, OREGON

Cover and interior design by Studio Gearbox
Cover photo © Vector pro / Shutterstock

Published in partnership with Brentwood Studios.
BrentwoodStudios.net

Need to Know for Graduates
Copyright © 2022 by Jeff Atwood
Published by Harvest House Publishers
Eugene, Oregon 97408
www.harvesthousepublishers.com

ISBN 978-0-7369-8131-6 (hardcover)
ISBN 978-0-7369-8132-3 (eBook)

Printed in Colombia

23 24 25 26 27 28 29 30 / NI / 10 9 8 7 6 5 4 3

TO ALL THE TEACHERS IN MY FAMILY

I come from a long line of teachers. Amazing people who have committed their lives to prepare and educate students across the country. They have taught students in one-room country schoolhouses, university classrooms, suburban elementary schools, and everything in between.

Thanks to you, Dad, Jackie, Grandma, Ann, Jane, Mary, and so many more who shared with me and countless others the importance of learning and leading.

INTRODUCTION

Congratulations on your graduation! This is one of most important transitions you will ever have. It is the tipping point between preparation and possibility. This day is the culmination of years and years of blood, sweat, and tears, and the only tangible reward is a diploma that will ultimately end up in the bottom of a box in your parents' attic. The real reward of graduation is not a look back at the past, but rather the opportunity to look ahead at the wide-open prairie that is your life.

You were made to do great things, things that only you can do.

Now go do them.

MY "NEED TO KNOW"

If you are giving this book as a gift to a friend or family member, you know full well that there's a lot more they need to know than what is written on these pages. Please take a minute to share advice you think the recipients of this book need to know about how to handle what lies ahead.

The same applies to you, the reader of this book. Please take a moment to write down some ideas or experiences you want to remember so you can share them with future graduates.

_____

_____

_____

_____

_____

_____

YOU ARE LOVED.
ALWAYS. FOREVER.
NO MATTER WHAT.
NOTHING COULD
EVER CHANGE THAT.
EVERYTHING YOU NEED TO KNOW
IS SECONDARY
TO KNOWING YOU ARE LOVED.

SAY "I'M SORRY" FIRST.
AS SOON AS POSSIBLE.
WHEN YOU'VE DONE SOMETHING WRONG
OR HURT SOMEONE,
YOU CAN'T APOLOGIZE
FAST ENOUGH.

BE THANKFUL.
LOTS OF GOOD PEOPLE
DO LOTS OF GOOD THINGS
FOR YOU EVERY DAY.
MAKE SURE YOU
TELL THEM
THANK YOU.

**DON'T SPEND YOUR LIFE
WORRYING ABOUT THINGS
THAT MAY OR MAY NOT HAPPEN.
WORRYING DOESN'T
CHANGE THINGS.
DOING SOMETHING
CHANGES THINGS.**

YOU ARE NEVER COMPLETE.
YOU ARE ALWAYS

"COMPLETING."

EVERY DAY YOU ARE BECOMING

MORE (OR LESS) OF THE THINGS

THAT MAKE YOU, YOU.

MEMORIES ARE THE
CURRENCY OF THE SOUL.
THERE WILL SOON BE A TIME
WHEN "I REMEMBER WHEN..."
WILL BE SOME OF THE
HAPPIEST WORDS YOU CAN SAY.

YOU CAN NEVER
BE TOO GENEROUS.
YOU WILL ALMOST
ALWAYS HAVE ENOUGH.
PROBABLY MORE THAN ENOUGH.
SO PLEASE GIVE
WHEN IT'S NEEDED
AND ALSO WHEN
IT'S UNEXPECTED.

TAKE A CLASS
OR START A HOBBY
THAT MAKES YOUR PARENTS SAY,
"WHY IS SHE DOING THAT?"

MAKE SURE YOU SPEND
LOTS OF TIME EXPLORING
AND WONDERING
AND PONDERING,
BECAUSE IT IS OFTEN
IN DOING THOSE THINGS
THAT YOU FIND
WHAT BRINGS YOU JOY.

GO EAT DINNER
WITH YOUR GRANDPARENTS.
ASK ABOUT THEIR
CHILDHOOD FRIENDS AND
HIGH SCHOOL GRADUATION
AND FIRST JOB.
MUCH OF WHO YOU ARE
COMES FROM WHO THEY ARE.

MAKE DECISIONS
AND TAKE ACTION.
CLEANING UP A MISTAKE
FROM HAVING DONE SOMETHING
IS ALMOST ALWAYS EASIER
THAN TRYING TO EXPLAIN
WHY YOU DID NOTHING.

DO WHAT BRINGS YOU JOY,
NOT WHAT BRINGS
YOUR PARENTS JOY
OR PAYS WELL
OR LOOKS IMPRESSIVE.
FIND THE THING
THAT BRINGS YOU JOY.
THEN EVERYTHING ELSE
WILL LIKELY TAKE
CARE OF ITSELF.

TELL YOUR FRIENDS
WHAT MAKES THEM GREAT.
AND NOT JUST
"YOU'RE SO FUNNY"
OR "I LOVE HOW YOU
DO YOUR HAIR."
TELL THEM HOW THEY
MAKE THE WORLD
A BETTER PLACE.

BRUSH YOUR TEETH.
HAVING TEETH
IS ALWAYS BETTER
THAN NOT HAVING TEETH.

WHEN YOU MUST
DELIVER BAD NEWS,
FACE-TO-FACE
CONVERSATIONS
ARE ALWAYS BEST.
A PHONE CALL
WILL DO IN A PINCH.
NEVER A TEXT
OR A TWEET
OR AN EMAIL.

WASH YOUR CLOTHES
ONE DAY BEFORE YOU
THINK YOU NEED TO.
NEVER LET A LACK OF
CLEAN UNDERWEAR
KEEP YOU FROM
AN ADVENTURE.

DON'T WASTE TIME COMPARING YOURSELF TO OTHER PEOPLE.

WHEN YOU DO,
YOU DEFINE YOURSELF
BY WHAT OTHERS CAN
OR CANNOT DO,
NOT BY WHO YOU ARE
AND WHY GOD PUT YOU
ON THIS PLANET.

SOMETIMES OPPORTUNITY
KNOCKS ON THE FRONT DOOR.
WHEN IT DOES, ANSWER WITH
A SMILE AND A CUP OF TEA.
BUT SOMETIMES YOU MUST
CHASE OPPORTUNITY
INTO THE DEEPEST,
DARKEST JUNGLE
AND TAKE IT DOWN
WITH AN ELEPHANT GUN.
BE READY TO DO BOTH.

DON'T LET PEOPLE
YOU DON'T KNOW
DEFINE OR SHAPE
YOUR VALUE.
YOU ARE NOT
THE SUM OF "LIKES"
OR "FRIENDS"
OR ANY OTHER
SOCIAL MEDIA AFFIRMATION.

LIFE IS NOT FAIR.
SO DON'T FUSS OR FRET
WHEN THINGS DON'T
TURN OUT FAIR FOR YOU.
THERE WILL ALSO BE TIMES
WHEN SOMETHING ENDS WELL
FOR YOU BUT ISN'T FAIR
FOR SOMEONE ELSE.
IN THE END, IT ALL SEEMS
TO BALANCE OUT.

BE NICE TO PEOPLE
WHEN THEY DON'T
DESERVE IT. AND NOT JUST
"I'M BARELY TOLERATING YOU" NICE.
BE REALLY NICE.
BECAUSE THERE WILL BE DAYS
WHEN YOU ARE THE ONE
NEEDING SOMEONE
TO BE REALLY NICE.

DON'T WORRY THAT YOU NEVER PLAYED THE CLARINET.

MANY SCIENTIFIC STUDIES
PROVE NO ONE EVER SAID,
"I WISH I'D BEEN A CLARINETIST."
SAME FOR ANY OTHER REGRETS.
DON'T STRESS ABOUT
WHAT YOU HAVEN'T DONE;
JUST DO WHAT YOU CAN DO NOW.

SOMEWHERE ON THIS PLANET,
THERE IS SOMEONE SMARTER
OR FASTER OR PRETTIER THAN YOU.
(NOT TRYING TO BE HARSH,
IT'S JUST MATH.)
IT'S OKAY TO NOT BE THE
BEST AT EVERYTHING.

IT'S IMPORTANT TO NOTE
THAT THE CONVERSE TO
THE PREVIOUS STATEMENT
IS ALSO TRUE. THERE WILL
ALWAYS BE SOMEONE
LESS SMART, LESS TALENTED,
OR SMELLIER THAN YOU.
BUT PLEASE DON'T FIND
COMFORT IN THAT, BECAUSE
THAT'S JUST PLAIN MEAN.

CURIOSITY IS THE
KEY TO SUCCESS.
ASKING "WHY" OVER AND OVER
WHEN YOU'RE EIGHTEEN
OR TWENTY-TWO OR THIRTY
IS NOT NEARLY AS AGGRAVATING
AS IT WAS WHEN YOU WERE THREE.

SOMETIMES ICE CREAM
IS THE ONLY THING THAT
WILL MAKE IT ALL BETTER.

ICE CREAM IS GOOD.

HEARTACHE IS BAD.

ICE CREAM > HEARTACHE.

GO SEE THE WORLD.

THE BIGGER YOUR
EXPERIENCES ARE,
THE BIGGER YOUR VIEW,
YOUR UNDERSTANDING,
AND YOUR APPRECIATION
OF THE WORLD WILL BE.

JUST SHOW UP.
OPPORTUNITY
ALWAYS FOLLOWS
AVAILABILITY.

TAKE PICTURES OF
ANYONE AND ANYTHING
BUT YOURSELF.
YEARS FROM NOW
YOU WILL STILL KNOW
WHAT YOU LOOK LIKE.
MAKE SURE YOU REMEMBER
THE PEOPLE AND EXPERIENCES
THAT GOT YOU HERE.

BE THE FIRST
PERSON TO CLAP
WHEN A PERFORMER FINISHES.
GOOD OR BAD,
IT DOESN'T MATTER.
THEY WORKED HARD AND
DESERVE A QUICK RESPONSE.

NEVER LOSE SIGHT OF
WHERE YOU CAME FROM.
YOU ARE THE SUM OF
GENERATIONS OF PEOPLE
WHO HAVE SHAPED
WHO YOU ARE AND
WHO YOU WILL BE.

GIVE SOMEONE AN UNEXPECTED COMPLIMENT

AT LEAST ONCE EVERY DAY. PEOPLE LIKE AND NEED COMPLIMENTS.

REMEMBER
THE GOOD AND THE BAD.
BOTH HAPPEN
EVERY DAY.
AND BOTH ARE
IMPORTANT.

TELL THE TRUTH.
ALWAYS.

THERE ARE TWO KINDS
OF PEOPLE IN LIFE.
"LIFE GIVERS" AND
"LIFE SUCKERS."
BE THE FIRST, AND
STAY FAR AWAY
FROM THE SECOND.

WHEN YOU MUST
MAKE AN IMPORTANT
DECISION, ASK YOURSELF,
"WHAT'S THE WORST THING
THAT COULD HAPPEN?"
IF THE ANSWER IS
"I MIGHT LAND IN QUICKSAND,"
THEN DON'T DO IT.
HOWEVER, IF THE ANSWER IS
"I'LL REALIZE I DON'T
LOOK GOOD WITH BLUE HAIR,"
THEN GO FOR IT.

DON'T BE AFRAID
TO ASK FOR HELP.
IT'S NOT A SIGN OF WEAKNESS
TO ADMIT YOU DON'T
KNOW EVERYTHING.
IT'S A SIGN OF BEING
SMART ENOUGH TO KNOW
WHAT YOU DON'T KNOW.

TEXT YOUR MOM AND DAD
FOR NO REASON
BUT TO SAY
"HEY"
OR
"I LOVE YOU."

HEARTACHE IS UNIVERSAL.
EVERYONE HAS SOME
INHERENT SADNESS
IN THEIR LIFE.
PROBABLY WAY MORE
THAN THEY'RE LETTING ON.
LOOK FOR WAYS
TO UNDERSTAND
PEOPLE'S STORIES.

SAY YES TO THINGS
IN YOUR LIFE
A LOT MORE OFTEN
THAN YOU SAY NO.
NO IS USUALLY EASIER,
BUT YES IS USUALLY BETTER.

WHEN YOU TRIP
OVER YOUR FEET
IN THE TARGET PARKING LOT,
JUST REMIND YOURSELF,
"I WILL NEVER SEE
THESE PEOPLE AGAIN."

**DON'T JUST
TELL PEOPLE
WHAT YOU CAN DO.
SHOW THEM
WHAT YOU CAN DO.**

USE THE MINUTES
BETWEEN CLASSES OR
BETWEEN MEETINGS WISELY.
INSTEAD OF "I'LL START WHEN
I HAVE A CHUNK OF TIME,"
USE YOUR "BETWEEN" TIME NOW
SO YOU'LL USE LESS
"CHUNK TIME" LATER.

USE AN ALMANAC
TO PLAN YOUR ROAD TRIPS.

IT'S OFTEN HELPFUL TO GET CONTEXT BY LOOKING OUTSIDE THE SMALL CONFINES OF YOUR PHONE SCREEN.

(THE SAME APPLIES TO DREAMING BIG DREAMS OR PLANNING BIG PLANS. YOU NEED TO SEE BEYOND THE SMALL BORDERS.)

**DON'T WHINE
OR MAKE EXCUSES.
EVEN IF IT WASN'T
YOUR FAULT
OR YOU DIDN'T
DESERVE IT.
JUST SUCK IT UP,
OWN THE ISSUE,
AND MAKE IT BETTER.
BOSSES WANT SOLUTIONS,
NOT EXCUSES.**

LIVE EACH DAY WITH AS MUCH
ENERGY AND ENTHUSIASM
AND INITIATIVE AS POSSIBLE
SO THAT WHEN YOU
LIE DOWN AT NIGHT,
YOU THINK THREE THINGS:

1. THAT WAS A GREAT DAY.

2. MY TANK IS EMPTY.

3. I'M THANKFUL FOR MY LIFE.

THERE IS NEVER "ENOUGH,"
SO PLEASE BE CAREFUL
ABOUT CHASING THINGS
AND MONEY
AND STUFF.

WORKING HARD IS ALMOST ALWAYS MORE IMPORTANT

(AND A BETTER DETERMINANT OF SUCCESS)

THAN HAVING GREAT IDEAS. GREAT IDEAS DIE WITHOUT HARD WORK. HARD WORK CAN ALMOST ALWAYS STAND ALONE.

ALWAYS HAVE AN
UMBRELLA NEARBY.
WALKING OR SINGING
OR DANCING IN THE RAIN
IS LOTS OF FUN.
FOR TEN SECONDS.
AFTER THAT, YOU'RE JUST A
WALKING, SINGING, DANCING,
MOSTLY MISERABLE,
SOGGY FOOL.

HAVE THREE GO-TO QUESTIONS
TO HELP PROPEL CONVERSATION
FORWARD WHEN YOU MEET
SOMEONE. GOOD OPTIONS INCLUDE

"TELL ME ABOUT WHERE YOU GREW UP,"

OR

"WHAT DID YOU DO ON YOUR LAST VACATION?"

OR THE CLASSIC

"TELL ME ABOUT YOUR FAMILY."

YOU'RE GONNA MAKE MISTAKES.
WE ALL DO.
DO NOT LET THE
PAIN OF THE MOMENT STOP YOU.
FAILURE SHOULD NOT DAMPEN YOUR DREAMS;
IT CANNOT STEAL YOUR SKILLS,
NOR SHOULD IT DIMINISH YOUR PASSION.

THE ONLY POWER THAT
FAILURE HAS IN YOUR LIFE IS TO
(OFTEN APPROPRIATELY)
SLOW YOU DOWN
OR, MORE OFTEN,
POINT YOU IN A BETTER DIRECTION.

LISTEN MORE
THAN YOU TALK.

LIKE, BY ABOUT A 60/40 RATIO,

OR EVEN BETTER, 70/30.

"LESS MOUTH, MORE EARS"

HELPS OTHERS KNOW

YOU VALUE THEM AND

WHAT THEY HAVE TO SAY.

YOU ARE THE BOSS OF YOU. DON'T LET ANYONE ELSE TRY TO MAKE YOU SOMEONE DIFFERENT FROM WHO YOU ARE.

DO SOMETHING
SPECIFIC AND TANGIBLE
TO MAKE THE WORLD
A BETTER PLACE.
DON'T STOP WITH
"I'M GONNA SIGN A PETITION" OR
"I'M GONNA WRITE A CHECK."
ACTION BEATS INTENTION EVERY TIME.

BE MOST
CONCERNED
ABOUT THE PERSON
RIGHT IN FRONT OF YOU.

MAKE LISTS.

LIFE CAN BE OVERWHELMING
IF YOU TRY TO
DIGEST TOO MUCH OR
DO EVERYTHING AT ONCE.
IF YOU DON'T STRUCTURE
YOUR LIFE AND YOUR TIME,
THEY WILL TAKE
CONTROL OF YOU.

LIFE IS FRAGILE.
THERE ARE NO GUARANTEES,
SO DON'T WAIT.

TRY NEW STUFF.

IF YOU NEVER GET IN A RUT,
YOU WILL NEVER NEED
TO GET OUT OF ONE.

**LEARN HOW TO
IRON YOUR CLOTHES.**
DON'T BE THE PERSON WHOSE
SCRUNCHED-UP SHIRT SCREAMS,
"YOU'RE NOT IMPORTANT ENOUGH
FOR ME TO KNOCK THE
TOP LAYER OF WRINKLES
OFF THIS SHIRT."

LAUGH AT YOURSELF.

YOU'RE GOING TO DO DUMB THINGS.
WE ALL DO. YOU CAN EITHER
WORRY ABOUT THE DUMB THINGS
OR LAUGH AT THEM.
LAUGHING IS MUCH MORE FUN.

LOOK PEOPLE IN THE EYE
WHEN YOU TALK TO THEM.
THEY WILL TRUST YOU MORE
AND BELIEVE THAT
WHAT YOU ARE SAYING
IS IMPORTANT.

MOVE FAST.

LONG AGO,

SOMEONE FAMOUS SAID,

"HE WHO HESITATES IS LOST."

THAT'S EVEN TRUER

TODAY THAN IT WAS THEN.

IN ORDER TO BE SUCCESSFUL,

YOU MUST BE ABLE TO

GATHER INFORMATION,

MAKE DECISIONS,

AND MOVE FAST.

WHEN YOU
TELL SOMEONE
"THANK YOU,"
REALLY SAY IT.
TAKE A MOMENT,
LOOK THE PERSON
IN THE EYE, AND
SAY THE WORDS
"THANK YOU."

COUNT YOUR BLESSINGS.
MAKE A LIST OF GREAT THINGS
HAPPENING IN YOUR LIFE.
IT'S EASY TO LOSE SIGHT OF
THINGS TO BE **THANKFUL** FOR
IF YOU DON'T PAUSE
TO REMEMBER THEM.

TO GIVE YOURSELF
SOME CONTEXT,
MAKE A LIST OF "EHH, WHATEVER"
THINGS IN YOUR LIFE
AND THEN A LIST OF
"THIS IS A DISASTER" THINGS.
I GUARANTEE YOU THE
GREAT THINGS WILL
FAR OUTNUMBER THE DISASTERS.

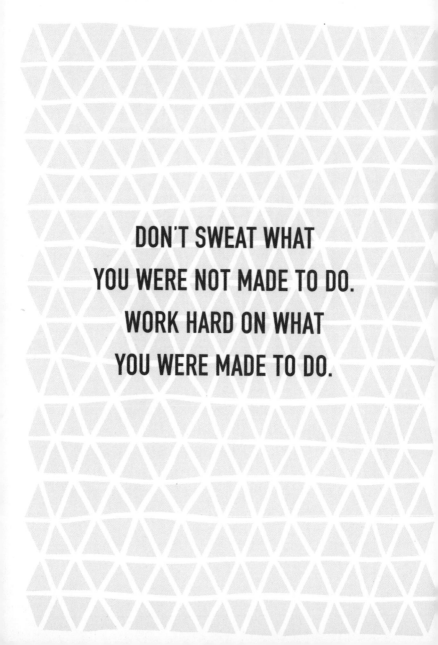

DON'T SWEAT WHAT
YOU WERE NOT MADE TO DO.
WORK HARD ON WHAT
YOU WERE MADE TO DO.

YOU ARE ONLY AS
GOOD AS YOUR WORD.
IF YOU SAID YOU WOULD
DO SOMETHING, DO IT.
NO MATTER HOW TIRED
OR COLD OR DISINTERESTED
OR (WORST OF ALL)
IF SOMETHING
BETTER COMES ALONG.
IF YOU SAID YOU WOULD DO IT,
DO IT.

LAUGH A LOT.
YOUR SMILE IS BEAUTIFUL,
AND YOUR LAUGH IS CONTAGIOUS.
LAUGH MORE, GRUMP LESS.

YOU OFTEN WIN BY LOSING.

YOU DON'T ALWAYS HAVE TO
BE 100 PERCENT RIGHT,
WIN EVERY ARGUMENT,
OR HAVE THE LAST WORD
IN EVERY DISAGREEMENT.
IT'S OKAY TO COME IN SECOND.

DON'T LET A MOMENT,
OR PEOPLE'S OPINION
OF YOU IN THAT MOMENT,
DEFINE YOU. YOU MUST LET
THEM BE WHAT THEY ARE—
THINGS THAT LAST A MOMENT.

**SURPRISE A WAITER
WITH A BIG TIP.**
IT DOESN'T HAVE TO BE CRAZY,
JUST ENOUGH SO THEY THINK,
"WOW, THAT WAS COOL."
**SOMETIMES A KIND GESTURE
CAN MAKE SOMEONE'S DAY.**

PLAY TO YOUR STRENGTH.
GOD MADE YOU TO BE
GOOD AT SOMETHING.
FIND THAT SOMETHING
AS FAST AS YOU CAN
AND DO IT MORE
THAN ANYTHING ELSE.

BE REALLY, REALLY,
REALLY, REALLY,
REALLY, REALLY, REALLY, REALLY,
CAREFUL ABOUT WHAT YOU
PUT ON SOCIAL MEDIA.
IT LASTS FOREVER.
REALLY.

MAKE "HOW CAN I HELP YOU"
PART OF YOUR DAILY VOCABULARY.
IF YOU SAY THAT INSTEAD OF
"I WANT [BLANK]" OR
"I NEED [BLANK]" OR
"I DESERVE [BLANK],"
THE WORLD AND YOUR LIFE
WILL BE BETTER FOR IT.

IGNORE YOUR CRITICS.

THE MORE SUCCESS YOU HAVE, OR THE HARDER YOU WORK, THE MORE LIKELY YOU ARE TO HAVE A CRITIC.

SOME CRITICS ARE JEALOUS.
THEY TRY TO BRING YOU DOWN
TO MAKE THEMSELVES FEEL BETTER.
SOME CRITICS ARE LAZY.
THEY COMPLAIN
HARDER THAN THEY WORK.

DON'T WORRY ABOUT PEOPLE
WHO ARE MORE INTERESTED
IN PULLING YOU BACK
THAN WISHING YOU WELL.

LIFE IS INCREMENTAL.
DON'T WAIT FOR PERFECT.
IT WILL NEVER COME.
IF STEVE JOBS HAD WAITED FOR
THE IPHONE TO BE JUST RIGHT,
WE'D STILL BE PUTTING
QUARTERS IN PAY PHONES.

LEARN HOW TO DRINK
YOUR COFFEE BLACK.
IT'S CHEAPER THAN ALL THAT
"HALF-CAFF FRAPPE" STUFF
AND BETTER FOR YOU TOO.
THIS IS NOT ONLY A
BEVERAGE SUGGESTION
BUT ALSO A
METAPHOR FOR SIMPLICITY.

TAKE THE LONG VIEW.

MAKE AS MANY DECISIONS
AS YOU CAN BASED ON
**WHAT'S BEST FOR
THE REST OF YOUR LIFE,**
NOT WHAT'S BEST FOR
THE REST OF THE WEEK.

LEARN HOW TO SCRAMBLE EGGS.
THEY ARE A MAGICAL FOOD,
BECAUSE WHEN YOU WHISK
EGGS AND MILK TO INFINITY,
THEY MAGICALLY BECOME
A PLATEFUL OF
RAINBOWS AND UNICORNS.

DON'T BELIEVE THE
GUIDANCE OFFICE POSTER
WITH PICTURES OF EAGLES
OR WATERFALLS THAT CLAIMS,
**"YOU CAN DO ANYTHING
IF YOU BELIEVE."**
NOT TO BE HARSH,
BUT IT'S SIMPLY NOT TRUE.
**INSTEAD, DO WHAT YOU CAN,
BE WHO YOU ARE, AND
TRUST GOD WITH THE REST.**

GO TO BED.

SLEEP IS IMPORTANT.

IT MAKES YOU

THINK MORE QUICKLY,

ACT LESS GRUMPY,

AND BE AN ALL-AROUND

NICER AND KINDER PERSON.

GO FIRST.

WE LIVE IN A

"YEAH, ME TOO" SOCIETY

WHERE PEOPLE TEND TO
AGREE WITH WHATEVER HAS
BEEN SAID OR DONE BEFORE.

YOU'RE MORE LIKELY TO

MAKE AN IMPACT WHEN

YOU MAKE THE FIRST MOVE.

BE FIVE MINUTES EARLY
RATHER THAN FIVE MINUTES LATE.
BEING EARLY SAYS
"I RESPECT YOU."
SHOWING UP LATE SAYS
"MY TIME IS
MORE IMPORTANT
THAN YOURS."

DON'T BE THE PERSON
WHO ALWAYS SAYS,
"I KNOW WE JUST STOPPED,
**BUT CAN WE
PLEEEEASE TAKE THE
NEXT EXIT?"**
(THIS IS LESS ABOUT
BLADDER FUNCTION
THAN ABOUT PLANNING AHEAD.
BUT IT'S A LITTLE BIT ABOUT
BLADDER FUNCTION TOO.)

TRY TO END EVERY CONVERSATION
IN SUCH A WAY THAT
IF YOU NEVER AGAIN
SPEAK TO THAT PERSON,
THEY WILL ALWAYS
THINK WELL OF YOU.

MONEY IS NOT EVERYTHING.

THAT'S NOT TO
SAY IT'S NOTHING.
IT'S JUST NOT THE EVERYTHING
SOME PEOPLE
MAKE IT OUT TO BE.

YOU DON'T HAVE TO
WIN ALL THE TIME.
YOU JUST DON'T.
THAT'S ALL THERE IS
TO SAY ABOUT THAT.

JUST BECAUSE YOU CAN

DOESN'T MEAN YOU SHOULD.

YOU CAN GET A TATTOO OF

JUSTIN BIEBER JUGGLING PINEAPPLES,

OR YOU CAN WALK THROUGH THE

DESERT WHILE WEARING PANTS

CROCHETED OUT OF TWIZZLERS.

IT DOESN'T MEAN YOU SHOULD.

PROCEED UNTIL APPREHENDED.
(THIS IS NOT LEGAL ADVICE, BUT
RATHER AN ENCOURAGEMENT TO
GET STARTED ON WHATEVER
YOU THINK YOU SHOULD START.)

DRINK MORE WATER.

SEVENTY-FIVE

PERCENT OF THE PLANET

IS COVERED BY WATER.

IF GOD HAD WANTED US TO DRINK SODA,

HE WOULD HAVE FILLED AT LEAST

ONE OF THE GREAT LAKES

WITH COKE.

**THE PAST IS PAST.
YOU CAN'T UNDO MISTAKES,
AND YOU SHOULDN'T
WALLOW IN WHAT-IFS.**

THE MORE YOU LIVE IN THE PAST,

THE MORE LIKELY YOU ARE

TO MISS THINGS IN THE NOW

AND THE YET TO COME.

WRITE THINGS DOWN.

IN A BOOK.

THE KIND THAT HAS

PAGES MADE OF PAPER.

YOU'LL THINK GREAT THOUGHTS,

AND THEY DESERVE TO BE

READ AND REMEMBERED.

GET TO KNOW PEOPLE
DIFFERENT FROM YOU.

IT WILL
HELP YOU KNOW
YOURSELF BETTER.

GIVE PEOPLE **YOU** IN THE MOMENT.
NOT YOU LOOKING AT YOUR PHONE.
NOT YOU WITH ONE EARBUD IN.
NOT YOU IMAGINING WHAT
YOU'RE GOING TO DO NEXT.
ALL **YOU.** ALL IN.
ALL THE TIME.

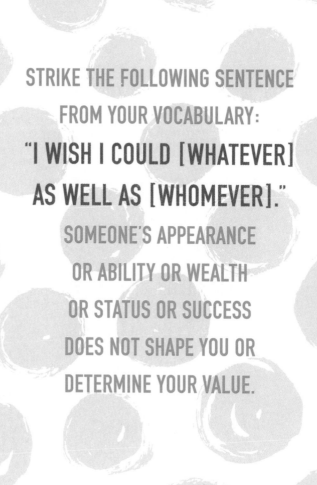

STRIKE THE FOLLOWING SENTENCE
FROM YOUR VOCABULARY:
"I WISH I COULD [WHATEVER]
AS WELL AS [WHOMEVER]."
SOMEONE'S APPEARANCE
OR ABILITY OR WEALTH
OR STATUS OR SUCCESS
DOES NOT SHAPE YOU OR
DETERMINE YOUR VALUE.

YOU CAN ALMOST
NEVER GO WRONG
EATING A
**WARM CHOCOLATE
CHIP COOKIE.**

ASK YOURSELF
ONE SIMPLE QUESTION
AT THE END OF EVERY DAY:
"DID I MAKE SOMEONE'S
LIFE BETTER TODAY?"
IF YES, THEN IT WAS
LIKELY A VERY GOOD DAY.
IF NO, THEN YOU HAVE SOMETHING
TO FOCUS ON TOMORROW.

A DOUBLE SHOT OF FEBREZE

IS NOT THE SAME THING AS

DOING LAUNDRY.

BE CAREFUL TO LEAVE

A LITTLE SPACE IN YOUR DAY

TO DO NOTHING.

LIFE IS HECTIC, AND

IF YOU'RE NOT CAREFUL,

IT WILL CLOSE IN AROUND YOU.

MAKE SURE YOU LEAVE

A LITTLE MARGIN

AROUND THE EDGES,

A MOAT TO PROTECT

YOUR SANITY.

THERE ARE VERY FEW "SNOW DAYS" IN REAL LIFE.

DON'T EVER LOOK LIGHTLY UPON THE GIFT OF FREE TIME.

LOYALTY MATTERS.

BE LOYAL,

AND BE WORTHY

OF LOYALTY.

DON'T ORDER
STEAK AT THE BEACH
OR SUSHI IN IOWA.

FISH IS FROM THE OCEAN,
AND COWS LIVE ON THE PRAIRIE.

GET THE STUFF THAT'S FROM

WHEREVER YOU ARE.

YOU CAN'T TELL PEOPLE
WHO ARE IMPORTANT TO YOU
THAT THEY ARE IMPORTANT TO YOU
OFTEN ENOUGH.
TELL THEM.
WITH YOUR WORDS.

PENNIES MATTER.

ALWAYS PAY ATTENTION

TO THE SMALL THINGS.

IT'S NEVER
TOO LATE TO START.
FIND THE MOST
INTERESTING THING IN YOUR
"WOULDA, COULDA, SHOULDA"
DRAWER, PULL IT OUT,
DUST IT OFF, AND
START. TODAY.

EVERY SIX MONTHS
ASK YOURSELF,
"AM I HEADED WHERE
I WANT TO GO?"
IF YES, THEN KEEP GOING.
IF NO, THEN ASK THREE
MORE QUESTIONS:
1. "WHERE AM I?"
2. "HOW DID I GET HERE?"
3. "HOW DO I GET OUT OF HERE FAST?"

IF YOU MAKE A MESS,
CLEAN IT UP.
THIS APPLIES EQUALLY
TO THE KITCHEN
AND RELATIONSHIPS.

ALWAYS AIM ONE STEP HIGHER
THAN THE "SUGGESTED DRESS"
ON AN INVITATION.
YOU NEVER WANT TO BE
THE PERSON WHO
MAKES PEOPLE ASK,
"DO YOU THINK
THOSE ARE PAJAMAS?"

NEVER STOP WONDERING.
ONCE YOU STOP TRYING
TO FIGURE THINGS OUT
OR MAKE NEW STUFF,
YOUR BRAIN WILL TURN
INTO A FUZZY HAIRBALL.
I'M NOT A SCIENTIST,
BUT THAT CAN'T BE GOOD.

EVERY NOW AND THEN
YOU WILL FACE
A SITUATION WITH
NO GOOD SOLUTION.
THERE IS ONLY "BAD CHOICE A"
OR "UGLY OPTION B."
ALL YOU CAN DO IS PICK
THE LEAST TERRIBLE SOLUTION
AND MOVE ON AS
QUICKLY AS POSSIBLE.

DON'T BE THE PERSON
WHO CARRIES A
SMELLY FISH SANDWICH
INTO A MEETING,
BECAUSE, WELL,
EWWWW...

**ALWAYS BE
ON THE LOOKOUT
FOR SOMEONE
WHO NEEDS HELP.**

**GOOD DEEDS CHANGE DAYS.
GOOD DAYS CHANGE LIVES.**

BE EASY TO TRAVEL WITH.
LIFE WILL BRING YOU
MANY MORE ADVENTURES
IF YOU ARE FLEXIBLE,
REASONABLE, AND
ACCOMMODATING.

GO TO FUNERALS.
THEY'RE OFTEN SAD
AND UNCOMFORTABLE, BUT MANY
TIMES PEOPLE JUST NEED TO BE
REMINDED THAT THE PERSON THEY LOVED
IS WORTH CELEBRATING.
BECAUSE THEY ARE.

"PLEASE" AND "THANK YOU"

ARE WAY UNDERRATED
AND UNDERUSED IN
EVERYDAY CONVERSATIONS.
PLEASE USE THEM IN
ALL YOUR CONVERSATIONS.
THANK YOU FOR READING THIS.

GIVE YOURSELF
DEADLINES ON DREAMS.
AT SOME POINT, YOU MUST
BEGIN TO GIVE SOME
TANGIBLE STRUCTURE AND
PROCESS TO YOUR DREAMS
TO BEGIN TO BRING THEM
INTO CLEARER FOCUS.
OTHERWISE THEY'RE JUST
WISHES, NOT DREAMS.

TIME = LOVE.
IT'S THAT SIMPLE.
YOU INVEST TIME
IN THE THINGS THAT
ARE IMPORTANT.
PEOPLE KNOW THAT
YOU CARE ABOUT THEM
BECAUSE YOU MAKE
THEM A PRIORITY.

YOU ARE THE SUM OF YOUR EXPERIENCES,

NOT THE SUM OF OTHERS' EXPECTATIONS. LET

WHAT YOU HAVE LEARNED AND WHAT YOU HAVE DONE AND WHAT YOU LOVE TO DO

GUIDE YOUR PATH.

WHEN YOU GO
TO LUNCH OR DINNER
WITH A FRIEND,
MORE OFTEN THAN NOT,
**BE THE PERSON WHO
PICKS UP THE CHECK.**
GENEROSITY AND HOSPITALITY
ARE HALLMARKS OF
A CIVILIZED SOCIETY.

**SPEND LESS
THAN YOU MAKE.**
EASIER SAID
THAN DONE.

FIND A HAT AND
A HOODIE YOU LOVE.
IF YOU CHOOSE WISELY,
THEY WILL BRING YOU
COMFORT FOR A LONG, LONG TIME
(AND ALLOW YOU TO SLEEP
TWO MINUTES LATER FOR CLASS).

EXPECT THE BEST FROM PEOPLE.

WE TEND TO LOOK FOR THE WORST
AND ARE SURPRISED
BY ANYTHING DIFFERENT.

TRY TO FIND THE KINDNESS
AND GENTLENESS
AND GOODNESS.

ONCE A SUMMER,
TAKE A FLYING LEAP
OFF THE DIVING BOARD
WHILE SCREAMING "CANNONBALL!"
AT THE TOP OF YOUR LUNGS.
LIFE IMMEDIATELY BECOMES
BETTER FOR EVERYONE
WITHIN EARSHOT.

KEEP PICTURES
OF PEOPLE YOU LOVE
AND MEMORIES YOU CHERISH
ON YOUR PHONE.
WHEN YOU'RE LONELY OR SAD,
**GOOD MEMORIES
CAN BRIGHTEN
YOUR DAY.**

MAKE YOUR PASSWORD
SOMETHING THAT
MAKES YOU SMILE.
YOU USE YOUR PASSWORD
A THOUSAND TIMES A WEEK.
GIVE YOURSELF A GIGGLE
EVERY TIME YOU LOG IN.

FINISH WELL.
FIRST IMPRESSIONS
ARE IMPORTANT,
BUT MORE LASTING IS
THE WAY THINGS END.
SPORTS FANS RARELY TALK
ABOUT THE FIRST POINTS
SCORED IN A GAME, BUT
THEY REMEMBER THE
FINAL SCORE.

**TURN OFF
THE LIGHTS
WHEN YOU
LEAVE A ROOM.**
YOU WOULDN'T LET
THE WATER RUN ALL NIGHT
OR TOSS PENNIES OUT THE
WINDOW WHILE YOU'RE
DRIVING DOWN THE ROAD.

DON'T TRUST JUST
ONE SOURCE FOR ANYTHING.
JUST BECAUSE A WEBSITE
SAYS SOMETHING IS TRUE,
DON'T BLINDLY ASSUME THAT IT IS.
ALWAYS DO YOUR OWN RESEARCH.

TELL YOUR SIBLINGS
THAT YOU LOVE THEM.
BECAUSE YOU DO.
YOU KNOW IT,
AND THEY KNOW IT.
BUT IT'S REALLY IMPORTANT
THAT YOU TELL THEM.
SO GO AHEAD AND DO IT.
NOW.

GOOD FRENCH FRIES
ARE AN ART FORM
UNTO THEMSELVES.
GIVE THEM THE HONOR
AND RESPECT THEY DESERVE.
THE SAME APPLIES
TO CHEESEBURGERS.

LEARN HOW TO PLAY
ONE SONG ON THE
HARMONICA OR BANJO.
YOU WILL CRUSH THE ROOM.

(YOU ONLY NEED TO KNOW ONE SONG,
BECAUSE WHO EVER SAID,
"I WANT TO HEAR MORE BANJO"?)